Leaving the Shade of the Middle Ground
The Poetry of F.R. Scott

Leaving the Shade of the Middle Ground
The Poetry of F.R. Scott

Selected
with an
introduction by
Laura Moss
and an
afterword by
George Elliott Clarke

LAURIER POETRY SERIES

WILFRID LAURIER
UNIVERSITY PRESS

Wilfrid Laurier University Press acknowledges the support of the Canada Council for the Arts for its publishing program. We acknowledge the financial support of the Government of Canada through the Canada Book Fund for our publishing activities. The editors acknowledge the EMIC (Editing Modernism in Canada) project for providing funding that assisted in the preparation of this volume.

Library and Archives Canada Cataloguing in Publication

Scott, F. R. (Francis Reginald), 1899–1985
  Leaving the shade of the middle ground : the poetry of F.R. Scott / selected with an introduction by Laura Moss and an afterword by George Elliott Clarke.

(Laurier poetry series)
Includes bibliographical references.
Issued also in electronic formats.
ISBN 978-1-55458-367-6

  I. Moss, Laura F. E. (Laura Frances Errington), 1969– II. Title. III. Series: Laurier poetry series

PS8537.C6A6 2011   C811'.52   C2011-903051-9

Type of computer file: Electronic monograph in ePub format.
Issued also in print format and another electronic format.
ISBN 978-1-55458-378-2

  I. Moss, Laura F. E. (Laura Frances Errington), 1969– II. Title. III. Series: Laurier poetry series

PS8537.C6A6 2011b   C811'.52   C2011-903053-5

Type of computer file: Electronic monograph in PDF format.
Issued also in print format and another electronic format.
ISBN 978-1-55458-379-9

  I. Moss, Laura F. E. (Laura Frances Errington), 1969– II. Title. III. Series: Laurier poetry series

PS8537.C6A6 2011a   C811'.52   C2011-903052-7

Cover image by Marian Scott: *Artifact*, 1970 (acrylic on canvas, 152.4 cm x 152.4 cm), National Gallery of Canada (no. 18759). Reproduced with permission. Cover design and text design by P.J. Woodland.

This book is printed on FSC recycled paper and is certified Ecologo. It is made from 100% post-consumer fibre, processed chlorine free, and manufactured using biogas energy.

Printed in Canada

Here's a bomb to blast complacency, a wind to scatter the cobwebs of old conformities; a whip for knaves-in-office and a purge for hypocrites. Here's medicine for the strong and poison for the dull. Here's a rope to hang the canting chauvinist and a sword to arm the man who loves his country.

—Dust-jacket copy for *The Blasted Pine:
An Anthology of Satire, Invective and
Disrespectful Verse*

Table of Contents

Foreword

Early in the twenty-first century, poetry in Canada—writing and publishing it, reading and thinking about it—finds itself in a strangely conflicted place. We have many strong poets continuing to produce exciting new work, and there is still a small audience for poetry; but increasingly, poetry is becoming a vulnerable art, for reasons that don't need to be rehearsed.

But there are things to be done: we need more real engagement with our poets. There needs to be more access to their work in more venues—in classrooms, in the public arena, in the media—and there need to be more, and more different kinds, of publications that make the wide range of our contemporary poetry more widely available.

The hope that animates this series from Wilfrid Laurier University Press is that these volumes help to create and sustain the larger readership that contemporary Canadian poetry so richly deserves. Like our fiction writers, our poets are much celebrated abroad; they should just as properly be better known at home.

Our idea is to ask a critic (sometimes herself a poet) to select thirty-five poems from across a poet's career; write an engaging, accessible introduction; and have another writer—in this case, George Elliott Clarke—write an afterword. In this way, we think that the usual practice of teaching a poet through eight or twelve poems from an anthology is much improved upon; and readers in and out of classrooms will have more useful, engaging, and comprehensive introductions to a poet's work. Readers might also come to see more readily, we hope, the connections among, as well as the distances between, the life and the work.

It was the ending of an Al Purdy poem that gave Margaret Laurence the epigraph for *The Diviners*: "but they had their being once / and left a place to stand on." Our poets still do, and they are leaving many places to stand on. We hope that this series helps, variously, to show how and why this is so.

—*Neil Besner*
General Editor

Biographical Note

Born in 1899 in Quebec City, Francis Reginald (Frank) Scott was a poet, editor, professor of law, and founding member of the Co-operative Commonwealth Federation (CCF). Educated at Bishop's, Oxford (where he was a Rhodes Scholar), and McGill, Scott spent his academic career teaching constitutional law in the McGill Faculty of Law (1928–68). He married the Montreal painter, muralist, art teacher (with Norman Bethune), and commercial artist Marian Dale in 1928, and together they had one son, Peter Dale Scott, who became a diplomat and poet. In 1977, F.R. Scott won the Governor General's Award for Non-fiction for *Essays on the Constitution*. An Anglo-Quebecer, Scott was also committed to being part of a bilingual and bicultural Canada. He worked toward this by doing (rather literal) translations of several prominent Quebec poets (including Anne Hébert and Hector de Saint-Denys Garneau) and by sitting on the Royal Commission on Bilingualism and Biculturalism (beginning in 1963).

One of the "Montreal Group" of poets of the 1920s driven to overturn the "state of amiable mediocrity and insipidity" of Canadian letters (Kennedy, Walter, and Scott 3), Scott spent five decades writing poetry and acting as a contributing editor to a series of key "little magazines," including *The McGill Fortnightly Review* (1925–27), *The Canadian Mercury* (1928–29), *Preview* (1942–45), and *Northern Review* (1945–56). With poet A.J.M. Smith, Scott co-edited what has been called the first Canadian modernist collection of poetry, *The New Provinces: Poems of Several Authors* (1936) (with work by E.J. Pratt, Robert Finch, Leo Kennedy, and A.M. Klein), as well as the acerbic collection of satire *The Blasted Pine* (1957). His first solo collection, *Overture* (1945), was followed by *Events and Signals* (1954), *The Eye of the Needle* (1957), *Signature* (1964), *Selected Poems* (1966), *Trouvailles* (1967), *The Dance Is One* (1973), and the Governor General's Award–winning *The Collected Poems of F.R. Scott* (1981).

Scott was not only a poet and a law professor but also an advocate of social democracy. He responded to the economic ruin of the 1930s Depression by joining historian Frank Underhill and others to form the League for Social Reconstruction (LSR). Together, they united with labour groups and farmers to create the CCF, which Scott served as national chair for eight years (1942–50). He was subsequently involved in the transition of the CCF to the New Democratic Party (NDP) in 1961. As an engaged public intellectual he criticized institutional structures and as a public poet he suggested new ways of approaching the socially just Canada he imagined. And yet his work is also often playful and witty on the one hand and gravely concerned with the legacy of loss and the fragility of both humanity and the environment on the other. Scott shared a strong commitment to leftist politics with several other important Canadian writers of his day, including Klein, Kennedy, Irene Baird, Dorothy Livesay, Anne Marriott, and Earle Birney. Upon Scott's death in Montreal in 1985, the poet Louis Dudek declared that his passing marked the end of an era.

Introduction

There is an ice-breaking game where participants have to list five people they'd like to have dinner with and then explain why. I have rarely played this game when someone hasn't said Albert Einstein or Mother Teresa. As much as I respect these two historical figures, they aren't on my list. I'd rather have a real wrangling conversation than the respectful fawning and series of awkward silences I suspect would ensue at a dinner with Einstein or the lazy guilt I'd feel at a dinner with Mother Teresa. One of my five is the poet F.R. Scott. He has the marks of a good dinner companion—wit and a sharp tongue; a passionate commitment to art and politics; a long life full of stories, friendship, and influence; and the ambivalent experiences of being a public and counter-public poet. I would like to ask him what it was like living in Montreal in the 1920s and being cocky enough to try to reform Canadian poetry; in the Depression of the 1930s, fervently planning a democratic-socialist future for the nation while struggling to get a collection of formally innovative, socially minded poetry published; in the 1940s, during a war he saw as driven by capitalism, surrounding himself with a burgeoning poetry scene that had its own heroic dramas; in the 1950s, reassessing Canadian identity and the role culture played in it; in the 1960s, taking part in the Royal Commission on Bilingualism and Biculturalism and hosting poetry evenings in his Montreal living room with poets moving between French and English; and then, in the 1970s, finding that he had come to be viewed by the younger generation of nationalists and postmodernists as a venerable figure of the Establishment he had spent his life kicking against.

I'd love to ask Scott about his trip with Pierre Trudeau to the Mackenzie River ("testing his strength / against the strength of his country" ["Fort Smith"]) and his lifelong friendship with A.J.M. Smith, about his legal defence of D.H. Lawrence's novel *Lady Chatterley's Lover* against charges of obscenity in the Supreme Court of Canada (see "A Lass in Wonderland"), and about his deep involvement with the Co-operative Commonwealth Federation (CCF). I'd ask what he thought of Leonard Cohen's jazz recitation recording of "Villanelle for Our Time" on his album *Dear Heather* (2004). I'd want to tell him that his poems "All the Spikes But the Last" and "Laurentian Shield" make my students sit up and take notice. Scott's life and my own overlapped by a few years, and I believe we lived just a few blocks away from each other when I was a small girl and he was an older man. I imagine we waited at the same light once or twice to cross Sherbrooke Street together. I suspect he waved to me out a car window. At dinner I'd want to compare his Montreal with mine. Mostly, however, I'd want to engage with the poet whose work often, not always but often, gets me in the gut as well as in the mind, and whose art keeps me rethinking my relationships with place, power, privilege, and people.

Born in Quebec City in 1899, Scott was an important figure in both avant-garde art and politics in Canada through the twentieth century. As a poet, editor, constitutional lawyer, and teacher, he was an outspoken advocate of change. In 1931 he explained his position: "the modernist poet, like the socialist, has thought through present forms to a new and more suitable order. He is not concerned with destroying, but with creating, and being a creator he strikes terror into the hearts of the old and decrepit who cannot adjust themselves to that which is to be" ("New Poems" 338). This is the crux with Scott: he wanted to "make it new" (à la Ezra Pound) in Canadian poetics and he wanted to make Canada new through socialism. In a 1950 address, Scott unequivocally joins economic and aesthetic factors as prime contributors to the "potential social evolution in Canada's northland," arguing that "we can create a beautiful social language through our daily work of making and building a society, and in this sense the social order is a work of art and we ourselves are the artists" (qtd. in Bentley 28–29).

The urgency of his mandate for change is evident in Scott's early poem "Overture" (first published in *Canadian Forum* in 1934 and later the title poem of his first solo collection in 1945) and echoes throughout his career:

But how shall I hear old music? This is an hour
Of new beginnings, concepts warring for power,
Decay of systems—the tissue of art is torn
With overtures of an era being born.

This is the hour, now. Against what he viewed as the built-in mediocrity of the status quo, Scott advocated a rethinking of structures of poetry, of law, and of government. To do this he targeted inherited forms of poetics, of jurisprudence, and of governance that lock people into processes of behaviour and thought, and he argued the need to counter accepted rules and forms. As Candida Rifkind notes, "despite his resistance to orthodoxy, however, Scott sought solutions in orthodox places: Parliament, the courts, political organizations and parties, democratic periodicals, and other institutions of the public sphere" (86).

In this vein, in the early 1930s, alongside his work as a professor of consti-
tutional law at McGill University, Scott joined Frank Underhill, Eugene
Forsey, and E.A. Havelock, among others, to form the League for Social
Reconstruction (LSR). In 1933 they were instrumental in preparing the Regina
Manifesto (adopted by the CCF at its first national convention), which
declared that "No C.C.F. Government will rest content until it has eradicated
capitalism and put into operation the full programme of socialized planning"
(Lewis and Scott 122). Following his stint as the national chairman of the CCF
from 1942 to 1950, Scott was involved in the transition of the CCF to the NDP
(New Democratic Party) in 1961. With the CCF, Scott advocated social welfare
initiatives such as socialized health and dental services and publically organ-
ized health, unemployment, accident, and health insurance; "social owner-
ship" of national industries, resources, and public utilities; and "foreign policy
designed to obtain international economic cooperation and to promote disar-
mament and world peace" (Lewis and Scott 204). The social vision of the CCF
was clearly part of Scott's perspective on law as well. In a series of CBC Radio
lectures on the Canadian Constitution and Human Rights, broadcast in 1959,
Scott "assessed the historical legacy of human rights in Canada, and proposed
the creation of a charter of rights entrenched in the written constitution"
(Toope 171). Indeed, the Canadian Charter of Rights and Freedoms was
entrenched in the Constitution in 1982. In several facets of his career, Scott
actively challenged public institutions and pushed reform. As he comments in
1942, the "duty of the poet is to help in the enfranchisement, not to decorate
the ancient chariot" ("A Note" 5). Rifkind observes that "his irony was mili-
tant, but his vision, grounded in the Fabian reformist spirit of the modern
social sciences, was not" (86).

Defending his active political career and his outspokenness (considered
uncomely by some of his peers and as class betrayal by others) in "To Certain
Friends," Scott extols his readers to consider what happens if you "leave the
shade of the middle ground" to "walk in the open air" toward "definite
action." He criticizes certain friends for having idealism that fails to meet
pragmatism and for fearing "the positive formation of opinion." Scott is ven-
omous in criticizing Prime Minister William Lyon Mackenzie King
(1874–1950), in "W.L.M.K.," for failing to take "shape / Because he took no
sides" and for choosing rather to "postpone, postpone, abstain." The publica-
tion note for "To Certain Friends" in The Eye of the Needle clarifies, "a man
with an open mind, says D.H. Lawrence, is like a pipe open at both ends"
(69). While he worked diligently for a socialized collectivity, in his poetry he
also acknowledges the individuality of the artist: "for individuality / lies
beneath collectivity," as he writes in "My Amoeba Is Unaware," where "The I

of the self / is no less in them than in the entire colony." Or in "A Grain of Rice," where we see the wonder of the world in the insignificant single grain even as "science / Is equal of truth and of error."

Seldom refraining from taking a potentially unpopular and unsettling stand in politics, Scott urged poetry to do the same. As a young man he criticized what he termed the "mediocrity" of the poetry of the so-called "maple leaf school" (particularly that of the older generation of poets—Bliss Carman, Duncan Campbell Scott, Archibald Lampman, and Charles G.D. Roberts—whom he lambastes in "The Canadian Authors Meet"), and he implored his contemporaries to overhaul both the form and content of modern poetry. While attending law school at McGill University, Scott joined forces with fellow students in an attempt to revolutionize poetry in Canada. He, A.J.M. Smith, Leon Edel, Leo Kennedy, and A.M. Klein (now known as the "McGill Movement" or the "Montreal Group") did not see themselves as Canadians in isolation. They were also attracted to the modern poetry of the day in Great Britain and the United States. Scott identifies W.B. Yeats's (in his late poetry), Harriet Munro, editor of Chicago's *Poetry* magazine, and especially T.S. Eliot as particularly influential to his work. Scott was drawn to the modernist attention to form. This is evident in the wide range of formal play (particularly playful enjambment) in his work. It is also clear in his insistence on brevity and density and his removal of what he likely considered to be rhetorical excess. He often uses imagistic language and chooses concrete over abstract representations. Finally, Scott's poetry rarely wallows in the sentimentality he criticized so strongly in the previous generation of poets in Canada. In Scott's letter to E.J. Pratt of January 11, 1934, on *New Provinces* (the book that has been called the first collection of modernist poetry in Canada), Scott wrote: "We are not aiming at anything extraordinarily experimental, but so far as possible we would like to indicate that we are all post-Eliot. I wish we could introduce a touch of political radicalism somewhere." Over the course of his sixty-year career, while Scott experimented with a myriad of forms and rhythms (with a tendency toward free verse but with a substantial number of measured stanzas in his oeuvre), there is a remarkable consistency in his poetry in the interplay between thematic concerns and formal poetic choices—while criticizing institutional structures, he'll break a predicted line, for instance.

What Scott and other poets of his cohort in Canada (and those who sat outside his cohort, like Dorothy Livesay and Miriam Waddington) brought to modernism was a shared sense of leftist politics and a determination to decolonize Canadian culture. They drew from the Group of Seven artists a desire to create art that was specifically Canadian and that reflected the environment in expressionistic rather than realistic terms. Less concerned with the "Mystic North" than Lawren Harris, they created populated portraits of the Canadian landscape. In "Laurentian Shield" and "Trans Canada," for instance, and later in "Fort Smith" and "A New City: E3," Scott marks the impact of human development, colonization, and settlement history on the land, particularly in the North. (However, the phrase "Not written on by history, empty as paper" about the "inarticulate, arctic" has elicited criticism that "Laurentian Shield" erases the originary Aboriginal presence from Canada; others have responded that Scott begins with a notion of the land that predates any inhabitants.) We are left wondering what haunting "deeper note" is sounding in the mines and what further effect humans will have on the environment as "Man, the lofty worm, tunnels his latest clay, / And bores his new career." D.M.R. Bentley points to the poem "Fort Smith" to showcase Scott's "disturbing catalogue of the architectural structures that embody the process of economic, religious, bureaucratic, social, and cultural colonization" in northern development (although he deems Scott's Mackenzie River poems—including "Fort Smith" and "A New City: E3"—to "contain a combination of insight and lugubriousness as they further chronicle the manifestations and ramifications of the flow of people and materials into and out of the North") (34). Scott's poems reverberate with questions about the complex interdependence of humans, animals, ecosystems, and the non-human world ("Mural," "Orangerie," and "Incident at May Pond," for instance) and grapple with the "need for biojustice" in evolution and science ("My Amoeba Is Unaware").

Alongside socialist politics and attention to nature, Scott's poetry projects a kind of humanism that is aligned with the Universal Declaration of Human Rights: the affirmation of the dignity and common worth of all people, governed by a belief in self-determination. Scott reconciles socialism with this kind of humanism in the description of the shared space of the office in "On Saying Goodbye to My Room in Chancellor Day Hall," in which the Declaration of Human Rights hangs near the "left-wing manifestos." Scott's bare-bones beliefs are well illustrated in his short poem "Creed":

The world is my country
The human race is my race
The spirit of man is my God
The future of man is my heaven.

Such a creed transcends nationality, race, and religion in favour of an undifferentiated humanism for the unnamed speaker. The shared nature of joy and grief in a recognition of dignity are evident in "On Kanbawza Road," as the poem celebrates the transcendence of cultural difference when a "giant" bows to a child, and in the elegiac "On the Death of Gandhi," in the suggestion that "The doors of his temple have opened on all the world." Scott can also be less general and more particular: "Picture in 'Life,'" for example, highlights the potential complexities of dehistoricized travel and presumed knowledge. Although Scott spent sixty years being incredulous of master narratives, it seems that the "everything" that gets questioned in his poetry often stops at a universal humanist vision of equality (unlike the postmodern and postcolonial thinkers who come after Scott who wonder whose version of "everything" dominates).

Scott was unapologetic about writing poetry with what often amounted to a sharply political message. Without a blush, he countered criticisms about being preachy (as poet Irving Layton called him), prescriptive, programmatic, or even safely pedantic from his middle-class perch, with further determined poems about public accountability and counter-public innovations. Over the course of his long career, his political stand and his poetic sensibility fell in and out of critical favour. In a retrospective on the significance of Scott's social vision, F.W. Watt argues that Scott's voice sometimes "has its godlike, arrogant tones, it allows little room for subtle resonances, differing judgments or ambivalent feeling. Readers may feel that it sometimes goes beyond (or falls short of) making us *see*, and is pressing us to *do*, as it were from above" (qtd. in Campbell; italics in original). And yet critic Wanda Campbell has noted the pervasiveness of ambiguity in Scott's poetry that might lead us to ask, "Do" what? While we are implored to step out of the shade of the middle ground, we are not necessarily told in what direction to turn (although I suspect it would often be to the left). Campbell lists "some of the particularly ambivalent relationships that permeate Scott's poetry" as the "relationship between religion and science, the individual and the collective, language and liberty, and finally, the satiric target and the Utopian ideal" (1). Indeed, in the note on "Mural" in *Eye of the Needle*, Scott equivocates, "this is as near as I can get to a credible Utopia" (70). While Scott's art was driven by a social vision, his poems don't prescribe how to get there.

Often Scott's social vision takes the form of satire or "inverted positive statement." By criticizing something, you recommend its opposite as a solution. In their introduction to *The Blasted Pine: An Anthology of Satire, Invective and Disrespectful Verse Chiefly by Canadian Writers*, co-editors Scott and Smith present the standard definition of satire as "a method of exposing folly to the ridicule of reasonable men and vice to the condemnation of virtuous and responsible men," with a qualification (xv). It is the "intensity, bitterness, and passion" that are the "qualities by which excellence of satire and invective is to be measured" (xvi). *The Blasted Pine* includes several of Scott's own intense, bitter, and passionate satires (I include several in this volume) in sections fittingly titled with his own skewer point of criticism. In the "True Patriot Love" section, we find his now-canonical "W.L.M.K." and "Bonne Entente"; in "The Purse-Proud Prelate" we see "Brébeuf and His Brethren"; "The Canadian Authors Meet" headlines the "Indigenous Throstles" section; the ironic "Solid Citizens" section encompasses "Saturday Sundae" and "The Canadian Social Register"; and "Lest We Forget," written in response to World War One, is poignantly nestled in among the anti-war poems of "We Stand on Guard." The "destructive criticism" of satire prized by Scott is also evident in the "bombs to blast complacency" of his contemporaries included in *The Blasted Pine*—Smith, Klein, Pratt, P.K. Page, and Robert Finch, as well as the young bucks Irving Layton, Raymond Souster, Earle Birney, and those disrespectful and passionate satirists of previous generations Stephen Leacock, Alexander McLachlan, Robert Service, and even Archibald Lampman—whose "To a Millionaire" (1900) and the dystopic "The City of the End of Things" (1899) are important Canadian precursors to Scott's social criticism.

One of Scott's favoured forms of satire is the "trouvaille," or found poem, where he lifts phrases and fragments from public spaces—newspapers, signs, conversations—and reinscribes them in poetic form to highlight their absurdity, their beauty, or their humour. Poet Louis Dudek, in the introduction to Scott's collection *Trouvailles*, notes that Scott's "satirical poetry naturally turns on the absurdity of our social reality, aiming at enlightenment and imaginative improvement. All found poetry and found objects either discover deficiency or virtue where it might be least expected in the real" (3). The element of surprise is key for a poet like Scott, who demands an active reader/ listener. His poem "Bonne Entente," for instance, is composed of quotations from a newspaper, a building notice, and a menu. "Martinigram" is an accreditive overheard conversation. "The Canadian Social Register" ridicules the self-fashioning of the elite in an amalgamation of quotations from a prospectus for an aristocratic register. "The Robinson Treaties" uses the words of the original treaties, verbatim, to draw attention to the injustices of treaties negotiated under the Indian Act. "Ushering in the Quiet Revolution" is pure quotation from the "Quebec Liberal Party Campaign pamphlet giving qualifications for the election of 1960." Without adding a word himself beyond the pointed title about the inevitability of change, Scott marks the inextricable connections between religion and politics in the party and in the province.

Although the objects of desire for political change may have shifted slightly today, Scott's committed political contestation and artistic response to a litany of social problems, as well as his emphasis on the environment, are remarkably pertinent now. Scott weighed in on many of the issues important to current Canadian readers using some different terms but with no less urgency: biopolitics, neo-liberalism, environmental concerns (consider the prescience of "Mural" and genetic modification), freedom of speech and civil rights, human rights, and immigration.

Recently when I was teaching "All the Spikes but the Last," a student expressed real surprise that such a critical poem could have been published in 1957. "It just seems so connected to today's politics," he commented. The poem responds to E.J. ("Ned") Pratt's national epic poem about the construction of the railway "Towards the Last Spike" (1952). Scott acknowledges the significance of the Chinese labourers (ironically employing the derogatory term "coolies") who formed a significant portion of the workforce that constructed the railway. Upon completion of the construction, the Canadian government responded to concerns about the availability of Chinese workers to work in dangerous conditions for lower pay than Canadian workers by issuing the Chinese Head Tax ($50) as part of the Act to Restrict and Regulate Chinese Immigration to Canada. Scott points to the injustice of the Head Tax and of Pratt's retrospective erasure of the workers' presence. The student who was so attracted to this poem argued that it opened up an alien Canadian past to him. He had learned about the Head Tax and felt sickened by its hypocrisy and exclusion, but on reading this poem he realized that Canada was probably more complex than the explicitly racist legislation made it seem. This wasn't about revising history to retrieve the "just white man" who saw the evils of his compatriots, but it was one example for this student of how not every Canadian has always embraced government policy or the building of mythological national narratives. In this light, Scott's poetry offers contemporary readers a way past the middle ground into the cultural complexities of Canadian immigration policy, socialism in Canada, and the intersections of art, history, and politics.

The poems selected here represent a range of works spanning Scott's career as a poet. Because Scott often reworked and republished his poems multiple times, I have consulted the originals but have largely chosen to use the versions in his *Collected Poems* (with the notable exception of the inclusion of the final cancelled stanza of "The Canadian Authors Meet" from 1927, although I have adhered to the later version in all other aspects of the poem— for instance using the word "maple" rather than the original "lily" in the sixth stanza). The dates in brackets following each poem are of first book publication with two exceptions. "The Canadian Authors Meet" is noted as 1927, 1936, and 1945 to signal the revisions to the poem in each iteration from the *McGill Fortnightly* to *New Provinces* to *Overture* where, as Dean Irvine notes, the figure of the poet, the "very picture of disconsolation," from the final stanza "in the midst of cultural transition is lost in revision" (2). The poems that are here entitled "Social Notes I, 1932" and "Social Notes II, 1935" were originally published in *Canadian Forum* in May 1932 and March 1935, respectively. They appeared, in different section order under the single title "Social Notes," in *Overture* and *The Eye of the Needle* and finally in *The Collected Poems* in the order I have included here.

The Laurier Poetry Series normally asks the poet to write an afterword to the selection. Since this was not possible in this case, I wondered who might be a contemporary version of Scott—a public and counter-public poet who writes with beauty and irreverence. I am glad that George Elliott Clarke took up my invitation to step into Scott's position here. He insisted that "Miranda" and "Orangerie" be included. Productively, we read Scott and his poetry rather differently. I think I'll invite George Elliot Clarke to my imaginary dinner with F.R. Scott, and then I suspect I could create my own fiery poetic trouvaille.

—Laura Moss

Works Consulted

Bentley, D.M.R. "'New Styles of Architecture, a Change of Heart'? The Architexts of A.M. Klein and F.R. Scott." *The Canadian Modernists Meet.* Ed. Dean Irvine. Ottawa: U of Ottawa P, 2005. 17–58. Print.

Boire, Gary. "'Canadian (Tw)ink: Surviving the White-Outs.'" *Essays on Canadian Writing* 35 (1989): 1–16. Print.

Campbell, Wanda. "The Ambiguous Social Vision of F.R. Scott." *Canadian Poetry: Studies, Documents, Reviews* 27 (1990): 1–14. Print.

Djwa, Sandra, and R. St. J. Macdonald, eds. *On F.R. Scott: Essays on His Contributions to Law, Literature, and Politics.* Kingston: McGill-Queen's UP, 1983. Print.

Dudek, Louis. Introduction. Scott, *Trouvailles* 1–3.

Dudek, Louis, and Michael Gnarowski, eds. *The Making of Modern Poetry in Canada.* Toronto: Ryerson, 1967. Print.

Gnarowski, Michael. Introduction. *New Provinces: Poems of Several Authors.* Ed. Gnarowski. Toronto: U of Toronto P, 1976. vii–xxxii. Print.

Harris, Lawren. "Revelation of Art in Canada." *Canadian Theosophist* 15 July 1926: 85–88. Print.

Irvine, Dean. Introduction. *The Canadian Modernists Meet.* Ed. Irvine. Ottawa: U of Ottawa P, 2005. 1–13. Print.

Kelly, Peggy. "Politics, Gender, and New Provinces: Dorothy Livesay and F.R. Scott." *Canadian Poetry: Studies, Documents, Reviews* 53 (2003): 54–70. Print.

Kennedy, Leo, Felix Walter, and F.R. Scott. Editorial. *Canadian Mercury* 1 (1928): 3. Print.

League for Social Reconstruction. *Social Planning for Canada.* Toronto: T. Nelson, 1935. Print.

Lewis, David, and F.R. Scott. *Make This Your Canada: A Review of C.C.F. History and Policy.* Toronto: Central Canada, 1943. Print.

Morley, J.T. "Co-operative Commonwealth Federation." *The Canadian Encyclopedia.* Historica-Dominion, 2010. Web. 15 Sept. 2010.

Quiring, David. *C.C.F. Colonialism in Northern Saskatchewan.* Vancouver: U of British Columbia P, 2004. Print.

Rifkind, Candida. *Comrades and Critics: Women, Literature, and the Left in 1930s Canada.* Toronto: U of Toronto P, 2009. Print.

Scott, F.R. *The Canadian Constitution and Human Rights: Four Talks as Heard on CBC University of the Air.* Toronto: Canadian Broadcasting Corporation, 1959. Print.

———. *The Collected Poems of F.R. Scott.* 1981. Toronto: McClelland and Stewart, 1982. Print.

———. "Creed." *Collected Poems,* 89. Print.

———. *The Dance Is One.* Toronto: McClelland and Stewart, 1973. Print.

———. *Essays on the Constitution: Aspects of Canadian Law and Politics.* Toronto: U of Toronto P, 1977. Print.

———. *Events and Signals.* Toronto: Ryerson, 1954. Print.

———. *The Eye of the Needle: Satire, Sorties, Sundries.* Montreal: Contact, 1957. Print.

———. Letter to E.J. Pratt. 11 Jan. 1934. *The Complete Letters of E.J. Pratt: A Hypertext Edition.* Ed. David Pitt and Elizabeth Popham. Trent U, n.d. Web. 12 May 2010.

———. "New Poems for Old." *Canadian Forum* 11 (1931): 296–98, 337–39. Print.

———. "A Note on Canadian War Poetry." *Preview* 9 (1942): 5. Print.

———. *Overture.* Toronto: Ryerson, 1945. Print.

———. Preface. *New Provinces: Poems of Several Authors.* Ed. Scott and A.J.M. Smith. Toronto: Macmillan, 1936. Print.

———. *Selected Poems.* Toronto: Oxford UP, 1966. Print.

———. *Signature.* Vancouver: Klanak, 1964. Print.

———, trans. *St-Denys Garneau & Anne Hébert: Translations/Traductions.* Vancouver: Klanak, 1962. Print.

———. *Trouvailles: Poems from Prose.* Montreal: Delta, 1967. Print.

Scott, F.R., and A.J.M. Smith, eds. *The Blasted Pine: An Anthology of Satire, Invective and Disrespectful Verse.* Toronto: Macmillan, 1957. Print.

Stevens, Peter, ed. *The McGill Movement: A.J.M. Smith, F.R. Scott and Leo Kennedy.* Toronto: Ryerson, 1969. Print. Critical Views on Canadian Writers.

Toope, Stephen. "Cultural Diversity and Human Rights (F.R. Scott Lecture)." *McGill Law Journal* 42 (1997): 169–85. Print.

Trehearne, Brian. *The Montreal Forties: Modernist Poetry in Transition.* Toronto: U of Toronto P, 1999. Print.

Overture

In the dark room, under a cone of light,
You precisely play the Mozart sonata. The bright
Clear notes fly like sparks through the air
And trace a flickering pattern of music there.

Your hands dart in the light, your fingers flow.
They are ten careful operatives in a row
That pick their packets of sound from steel bars
Constructing harmonies as sharp as stars.

But how shall I hear old music? This is an hour
Of new beginnings, concepts warring for power,
Decay of systems—the tissue of art is torn
With overtures of an era being born.

And this perfection which is less yourself
Than Mozart, seems a trinket on a shelf,
A pretty octave played before a window
Beyond whose curtain grows a world crescendo.

[1945]

Laurentian Shield

Hidden in wonder and snow, or sudden with summer,
This land stares at the sun in a huge silence
Endlessly repeating something we cannot hear.
Inarticulate, arctic,
Not written on by history, empty as paper,
It leans away from the world with songs in its lakes
Older than love, and lost in the miles.

This waiting is wanting.
It will choose its language
When it has chosen its technic,
A tongue to shape the vowels of its productivity.

A language of flesh and roses.

Now there are pre-words,
Cabin syllables,
Nouns of settlement
Slowly forming, with steel syntax,
The long sentence of its exploitation.

The first cry was the hunter, hungry for fur,
And the digger for gold, nomad, no-man, a particle;
Then the bold command of monopolies, big with machines,
Carving their kingdoms out of the public wealth;
And now the drone of the plane, scouting the ice,
Fills all the emptiness with neighbourhood
And links our future over the vanished pole.

But a deeper note is sounding, heard in the mines,
The scattered camps and the mills, a language of life,
And what will be written in the full culture of occupation
Will come, presently, tomorrow,
From millions whose hands can turn this rock into children.

[1954]

Coelacanth

I am an iamb
    because the bones of my social fish
were so precise
      I was meant to be embedded
      in the soft mud of my ancestors
or to be drawn on stone
        giving out words dreams ideas
        regular as ribs
crisp in the perfection of pattern
      dated
    a trilobite in limestone

But the earthquake came
   the sea-bottom cracked
      the floor rose to an island
no time for quiet death
   the tranquility of fossilization
these were mountain days
   a new language in birds
diaspora of dactyls
   iambs split to the core
    now my ancient frame
cries for the deeps of Zanzibar
    and is answered only by
      I AM

[1964]

Orangerie

Sprays of white blossom
open from buds
on my orange bush,
with small green fruit
crowding the same branches
while four whole oranges gleam
ready and ripe
bending their stems to earth
waiting the fall:
a simultaneity of birth, growth and death.
Looking more closely
I saw a tiny ant on a twig
rubbing his feelers together
and muttering
"Natural Selection! Natural Selection!"

And then I read in the *Scientific American*
of that myrmecophile beetle
Atemeles pubicollis
spending his summers being fed by
Formica ants
who adopt him
because he secretes a juice
irresistible to ants, and how
leaving these hosts
when winter comes
he moves out to the grass-lands
to find *Myrmica* ants
there repeating the process
of succulent secretion
so he will be dragged
to another brood chamber
where he will be fed
for another six months,

and sure enough
watching the migration
from nest to nest
I saw a confident beetle
trundling along
muttering
"Survival of the Fittest! Survival of the Fittest!"

[1973]

My Amoeba Is Unaware

of this poem in its favour, though it shares
in my totality. Like adverbs, it qualifies
that to which it is attached, adding
slowly, carefully, painfully, to my living.
Hosts pay for dinner though the guests
be uninvited, and symbiosis
is seldom equal. What most impresses me
is its immortality, and the "bigness of its littleness."
Truly a marvel of adaptation, equally at home in ponds or paunches
since the beginning of life, and a threat to religion, with
an ancestry older than all the gods. Not being oviparous,
and multiplying geometrically by diffusion of fission,
parent and child are the same. Such a conception
is wholly immaculate, needing no redemption.
Hence no one is born at the expense of another
and death is purely external, an accident
but not a law. Then, as its size
is the reverse of colossal, it seems as far removed
as a prowling space-ship, thus creating
a vastness and mythology in my internal universe
which makes me macroscopic. Too long
have the surfaces sufficed us. Beauty, we are mistaught,
is skin deep, and holy men, lonely in caves,
have tried to resist temptation
by dwelling on the viscera of women,
thus spitting at heaven and bespattering themselves.
I proclaim equal rights for the parts, the wonder
of interdependence, the worth
of the cellular proletariate whose ceaseless labour
builds the cathedrals of eyes and hands. I honour
the encyclopaedia of the pseudopodia. The I of the self
is no less in them than in the entire colony, for individuality
lies beneath collectivity. But as to a relationship
unsought by either side, there is need

for bio-justice. None need tolerate
invasion of frontiers, bacillary insurrections,
unicellular anarchy, though such zeal
be without evil. I am its good, it is not mine, and herein lies
the right of defence. Therefore though I praise
this protozoic ancestor,
I aim at its death with all my feeble weapons,
knowing I do not know if it still survives.

[1954]

Mural

When shepherds cease to watch their flocks
And tend instead bacterial stocks;
When farmers learn in chemic schools
To architect the molecules;
When all our food comes fresh and clean
From some unbreakable machine,
And crops are raised in metal trays
Beneath the ultra-violet rays;
When eggs are laid in numbered tens
Without the cluck of boasting hens,
And from the cool assembly-lines
Come wormless fruits and vintaged wines;
When honey drips in plastic cone
With none but a mechanic drone,
And vitamins by legal right
Are bedded in each measured bite;
When cloths are spun from glass and trees
And girls are clad with engine ease,
And men in rockets leave the ground
To fly the pole with single bound;
When ova swell in Huxleyan tubes,
Paternal sperm is sold in cubes,
And babies nuzzle buna taps
As sucklings now the unsterile paps;
When rules of health need not espouse
The ventral processes of cows,
And man is parasite no more
On some less clever herbivore;
When sheep and cattle graze at will
As decorations on the hill,
And all the natural creatures roam
As pets within their zoo-like home;
When by some microscopic means
Geneticists control the genes

And coloured skin and crinkly hair
Are choices for each bridal pair—
Then, on the Eden air, shall come
A gentle, low, electric hum,
Apotheosis of the Wheel
That cannot think and cannot feel,
A lingering echo of the strife
That crushed the old pre-technic life.
Then poverty shall be a word
Philologists alone have heard,
The slightest want shall know its fill,
Desire shall culminate in skill.
The carefree lovers shall repair
To halls of air-conditioned air
And tune-in coloured symphonies
To prick their elongated bliss.
Man shall arise from dialled feast
Without the slaughter of a beast;
His conscience smooth as metal plate
Shall magnify his stainless state;
His bloodless background shall be blest
With a prolonged, inventive rest.
All violence streamlined into zeal
For one colossal commonweal.

[1945]

Lakeshore

The lake is sharp along the shore
Trimming the bevelled edge of land
To level curves; the fretted sands
Go slanting down through liquid air
Till stones below shift here and there
Floating upon their broken sky
All netted by the prism wave
And rippled where the currents are.

I stare through windows at this cave
Where fish, like planes, slow-motioned, fly.
Poised in a still of gravity
The narrow minnow, flicking fin,
Hangs in a paler, ochre sun,
His doorways open everywhere.

And I am a tall frond that waves
Its head below its rooted feet
Seeking the light that draws it down
To forest floors beyond its reach
Vivid with gloom and eerie dreams.

The water's deepest colonnades
Contract the blood, and to this home
That stirs the dark amphibian
With me the naked swimmers come
Drawn to their prehistoric womb.

They too are liquid as they fall
Like tumbled water loosed above
Until they lie, diagonal,
Within the cool and sheltered grove
Stroked by the fingertips of love.

Silent, our sport is drowned in fact
Too virginal for speech or sound
And each is personal and laned
Along his private aqueduct.

Too soon the tether of the lungs
Is taut and straining, and we rise
Upon our undeveloped wings
Toward the prison of our ground
A secret anguish in our thighs
And mermaids in our memories.

This is our talent, to have grown
Upright in posture, false-erect,
A landed gentry, circumspect,
Tied to a horizontal soil
The floor and ceiling of the soul;
Striving, with cold and fishy care
To make an ocean of the air.

Sometimes, upon a crowded street,
I feel the sudden rain come down
And in the old, magnetic sound
I hear the opening of a gate
That loosens all the seven seas.
Watching the whole creation drown
I muse, alone, on Ararat.

[1954]

A Grain of Rice

Such majestic rhythms, such tiny disturbances.
The rain of the monsoon falls, an inescapable treasure,
Hundreds of millions live
Only because of the certainty of this season,
      The turn of the wind.

The frame of our human house rests on the motion
Of earth and of moon, the rise of continents,
Invasion of deserts, erosion of hills,
      The capping of ice.

Today, while Europe tilted, drying the Baltic,
I read of a battle between brothers in anguish.
      A flag moved a mile.

And today, from a curled leaf cocoon, in the course of its rhythm,
I saw the break of a shell, the creation
Of a great Asian moth, radiant, fragile,
Incapable of not being born, and trembling
      To live its brief moment.

Religions build walls round our love, and science
Is equal of truth and of error. Yet always we find
Such ordered purpose in cell and in galaxy,
So great a glory in life-thrust and mind-range,
Such widening frontiers to draw out our longings,
      We grow to one world
      Through enlargement of wonder.

[1954]

Incident at May Pond

(For Wassily and Estelle)

I put an ant upon a stick
And put the stick into the pond.
The vessel drifted in the wind
And straightaway I was captive too.

A helpless stowed-away ant scoured
His narrow deck to seek escape.
The ship was banged with mighty force
Upon the tendril of a reed.

It swung, and veered, and hit a stone,
Bounced up and down in ripple wave.
Ant clung aboard with cunning care
And searched the edges all around.

Ten feet from shore ship came to rest
Beside a log that made a dock.
A road was cleared to solid ground
But ant by now had laid a plan.

He leaped into the wavy sea
And swam with contradictory stroke,
Six walking feet upon the film
His Christlike body did not break.

I was enchanted by his skill,
His canny sense of where to go.
I felt exempted from the guilt
Of playing God with someone's life,

When suddenly there was a swirl
Beside his desperate flailing legs.
A minnow we had both forgot
Was lurking furtive underneath.

A second swirl, a splash, a plop,
Then utter silence everywhere,
And little rings of widening waves
Expanded outward to this poem.

[1964]

Miranda

Miranda's undiminished
By any sense of sin,
She does not circumscribe herself.
The thoughts her mind puts on

And all her pretty whimsies
Emancipated run,
She has no system but herself,
No ether but her own.

She's saner than September,
More single than the sky.
I do not think that someone
Could love her more than I.

I saw her on a Sunday
So maiden on a path
It was a peal of laughter
To understand her worth.

That night the thing that happened
Would set an aunt to stare:
We lay distinct as spinsters
Yet close as kisses are.

And on the Monday morning
By none but poplars seen
We hung our clothes on tree-tops.
Less maiden, but more mine,

We shared our joy in daylight
Beneath a leafy sun.
Perhaps there was a squirrel
Saw us—but he has gone.

[1926]

Trans Canada

Pulled from our ruts by the made-to-order gale
We sprang upward into a wider prairie
And dropped Regina below like a pile of bones.

Sky tumbled upon us in waterfalls,
But we were smarter than a Skeena salmon
And shot our silver body over the lip of air
To rest in a pool of space
On the top storey of our adventure.

A solar peace
And a six-way choice.

Clouds, now, are the solid substance,
A floor of wool roughed by the wind
Standing in waves that halt in their fall.
A still of troughs.

The plane, our planet,
Travels on roads that are not seen or laid
But sound in instruments on pilots' ears,
While underneath
The sure wings
Are the everlasting arms of science.

Man, the lofty worm, tunnels his latest clay,
And bores his new career.

This frontier, too, is ours.
This everywhere whose life can only be led
At the pace of a rocket
Is common to man and man.
And every country below is an I land.

The sun sets on its top shelf,
And stars seem farther from our nearer grasp.

I have sat by night beside a cold lake
And touched things smoother than moonlight on still water,
But the moon on this cloud sea is not human,
And here is no shore, no intimacy,
Only the start of space, the road to suns.

[1945]

To Certain Friends

I see my friends now standing about me, bemused,
Eyeing me dubiously as I pursue my course,
Clutching their little less that is worlds away.

Full of good will, they greet me with offers of help,
Now and then with the five-dollar bill of evasion,
Sincere in their insincerity; believing in unbelief.

The nation's needs are to them considerable problems.
Often they play no bridge nor sit at the movies,
Preferring to hear some expert discuss every angle.

They show great zeal collecting the news and statistics.
They know far more about every question than I do,
But their knowledge of how to use knowledge grows smaller and
    smaller.

They make a virtue of having an open mind,
Open to endless arrivals of other men's suggestions,
To the rain of facts that deepens the drought of the will.

Above all they fear the positive formation of opinion,
The essential choice that acts as a mental compass,
The clear perception of the road to the receding horizon.

For this would mean leaving the shade of the middle ground
To walk in the open air, and in unknown places;
Might lead, perhaps—dread thought!—to definite action.

They will grow old seeking to avoid conclusions,
Refusing to learn by living, to test by trying,
Letting opportunities slip from their tentative fingers,

Till one day, after the world has tired of waiting,
While they are busy arguing about the obvious,
A half-witted demagogue will walk away with their children.

[1945]

Social Notes I, 1932

PROLOGUE

"We see the rise, O Canada,
The true North, strong and free,
(Tralala-lala, tralala-lala, etc. . . .)"

I

NATURAL RESOURCES

Come and see the vast natural wealth of this mine.
In the short space of ten years
It has produced six American millionaires
And two thousand pauperized Canadian families.

II

THE NEW PHILANTHROPY

This employer, who pays $9 a week for a ten-hour day,
Is exceedingly concerned
Lest Mr. Bennett should adopt the dole,
And so ruin the morale of the workers.

III

SUMMER CAMP

Here is a lovely little camp
Built among Canadian hills
By a Children's Welfare Society
Which is entirely supported by voluntary contributions.
All summer long underprivileged children scamper about.
And it is astonishing how quickly they look healthy and well.
Two weeks here in the sun and air
Through the kindness of our charity subscribers
Will be a wonderful help to the little tots
When they return for a winter in the slums.

IV

XMAS SHOPPING

It is so nice for people to give things at Christmas
That the stores stay open every evening till ten,
And the shop-girls celebrate the coming of Christ
By standing on their feet fourteen hours a day.

V

MODERN MEDICINE

Here is a marvellous new serum:
Six injections and your pneumonia is cured.
But at present a drug firm holds the monopoly
So you must pay $14 a shot—or die.

VI

JUSTICE

This judge is busy sentencing criminals
Of whose upbringing and environment he is totally ignorant.
His qualifications, however, are the highest—
A college course in Arts,
A technical training in law,
Ten years practice at the Bar,
And membership in the proper political party.
Who should know better than he
Just how many years in prison
Are needed to reform a slum-product,
Or how many strokes of the lash
Will put an end to assaults on young girls?

VII

LAND OF OPPORTUNITY

This young Polish peasant,
Enticed to Canada by a CPR advertisement
Of a glorified western homestead,

Spent the best years of his life
And every cent of his savings
Trying to make a living from Canadian soil.
Finally broken by the slump in wheat
He drifted to the city, spent six months in a lousy refuge,
Got involved in a Communist demonstration,
And is now being deported by the Canadian government.
This will teach these foreign reds
The sort of country they've come to.

VIII

TREASURE IN HEAVEN

Many ecclesiastics and pious persons
Draw dividends from this Power Corporation
Which underpays its workers and overcharges its consumers.
Nevertheless the sayings of the Master are obeyed,
For verily there is no rust on a Public Utility privately owned,
And the moth doth not corrupt its Class A Preferred Stock.

EPILOGUE*

*"I believe in Canada.
I love her as my home.
I honour her institutions.
I rejoice in the abundance of her resources. . . .*

*To her products I pledge my patronage,
And to the cause of her producers
I pledge my devotion."*

[*Canadian Forum* 1932; 1945, 1981]

---

* From *My Creed*, issued by the Hon. H.H. Stevens, Minister of Trade and Commerce, New Year's 1931.

Social Notes II, 1935

The efficiency of the capitalist system
Is rightly admired by important people.
Our huge steel mills
Operating at 25 per cent of capacity
Are the last word in organization.
The new grain elevators
Stored with superfluous wheat
Can unload a grain-boat in two hours.
Marvellous card-sorting machines
Make it easy to keep track of the unemployed.
There isn't one unnecessary employee
In these textile plants
That require a 75 per cent tariff protection.
And when our closed shoe factories re-open
They will produce more footwear than we can possibly buy.
So don't let's start experimenting with socialism
Which everyone knows means inefficiency and waste.

II

MOTHERHOOD

Her travail now over
And her brood gone far away
This old woman of fifty
Must go charring at $2 a day.

III

Have you ever noticed
How many members of religious orders
Who have taken perpetual vows
Of poverty
And chastity
Now spend their time defending private property
And urging the poor to have large families?

IV

COMING HOME

The Soviet ship from Leningrad to London
Was called the Co-operation,
But to reach democratic Canada
I travelled by the Duchess of Richmond.

V

GREAT DISCOVERY

After ten years of research
This great scientist
Made so valuable a discovery
That a big corporation actually paid him $150,000
To keep it off the market.

VI

OBSERVATION

In tonight's newspaper
There were two protests:
One by an Archbishop
Against the spread of communism,
And one by an unemployed man
Who said his children were sleeping four in a bed
To keep warm.

VII

GOVERNMENT HELP

After the strike began
Troops were rushed
To defend property.
But before the trouble started
Nobody seems to have bothered
To defend living standards.

VIII

GENERAL ELECTION

There is nothing like hard times
For teaching the people to think.
By a decisive vote
After discussing all the issues
They have turned out the Conservatives
And put back the Liberals.

[*Canadian Forum* 1935; 1945, 1981]

Lest We Forget

The British troops at the Dardanelles
Were blown to bits by British shells
   Sold to the Turks by Vickers.
And many a brave Canadian youth
Will shed his blood on foreign shores,
And die for Democracy, Freedom, Truth,
With his body full of Canadian ores,
Canadian nickel, lead, and scrap,
Sold to the German, sold to the Jap,
   With Capital watching the tickers.

[1945]

For R.A.S. 1925–1943

He left the country that he loved so well,
Shawbridge, Piedmont, and the Tremblant runs,
And climbed to the centre of war by his own trail.
Barred from the easy virtue of enlistment
He fought a private battle for his chance to share the world's crisis.

On his way to the scenes of death, he met death.
Death reached out with an eagerness that matched his own.
Death violent, Atlantic, submarine.
The challenge so absolute was met absolutely.

It was as though there were special need to attend
To this boy's daring, as though if his will survived
We should survive too easily, win with too sudden success,
Win without understanding the fulness of our penalty.

He bore in his single hand the essence of our tragedy.

I tell you no one anywhere brought more than this.
Not the comrades who crouched shoulder to shoulder at Stalingrad,
Not Buerling, superb in his skill,
Nor the heroisms noted on the field of battle.

I write of him because he wished to write,
And because he had time only to pour
The table of his contents upon the historic water.

[1945]

W.L.M.K.

How shall we speak of Canada,
Mackenzie King dead?
The Mother's boy in the lonely room
With his dog, his medium and his ruins?

He blunted us.

We had no shape
Because he never took sides,
And no sides
Because he never allowed them to take shape.

He skilfully avoided what was wrong
Without saying what was right,
And never let his on the one hand
Know what his on the other hand was doing.

The height of his ambition
Was to pile a Parliamentary Committee on a Royal Commission,
To have "conscription if necessary
But not necessarily conscription,"
To let Parliament decide—
Later.

Postpone, postpone, abstain.

Only one thread was certain:
After World War I
Business as usual,
After World War II
Orderly decontrol.
Always he led us back to where we were before.

He seemed to be in the centre
Because we had no centre,
No vision
To pierce the smoke-screen of his politics.

Truly he will be remembered
Wherever men honour ingenuity,
Ambiguity, inactivity, and political longevity.

Let us raise up a temple
To the cult of mediocrity,
Do nothing by halves
Which can be done by quarters.

[1957]

The Canadian Social Register

(A Social Register for Canada was promoted in Montreal in 1947. On the
Advisory Committee were names like Rt. Hon. Louis St Laurent, Sir Ellsworth
Flavelle, Air Marshal Bishop, Rear-Admiral Brodeur, Hon. J. Earl Lawson,
Hartland Molson, and others. A Secret Committee was to screen all applicants.
All quotations in this poem are taken verbatim from the invitation sent out to
prospective members.)

Reader, we have the honour to invite you to become a "Member
    of the Social Register,"
For the paltry fee of $125 per annum.
This "work of art, done in good taste," and listing annually the
    "Notables of the Dominion,"
Will contain nothing but "Ladies and Gentlemen pre-eminent in
    the Higher Spheres,"
A list, indeed, of "First Families,"
Who are "the very fabric of our country."
Thus shall we "build up in the Nation's First Families
A consciousness of their role in the life of a civilized democracy."
Thus shall we bring "added dignity and profound significance
To our cultural way of life."
Through deplorable lack of vision, in times past,
Men who were "great Canadians, have everlastingly passed into
    oblivion,"
Leaving no "footprints on the sands of time."
Somehow, despite their pre-eminence, they have disappeared.
Shall we, through "tragic shortsightedness," let the leaders of this era
"Disappear into the realm of eternal silence?"
"Shall there be no names, no achievements, to hearten and
    strengthen on-coming generations in time of stress?"
If they have failed to make history, shall they fail to make The
    Canadian Social Register?
No—not if they can pay $125 annually,
And pass our Secret Committee.

For there is a "Secret Committee of seven members,"
Who will "determine the eligibility of those applying for
     membership."
Thus will the Social Register be "accepted in the most fastidious
     circles."
And to aid the Secret Committee you will send
The name of your father and the maiden name of your mother,
And the address of your "summer residence,"
(For of course you have a summer residence).
You may also submit, with a glossy print of yourself,
"Short quotations from laudatory comments received on diverse
     public occasions."
When printed, the Register will be sent,
Free, gratis, and not even asked for,
To (among many others) the "King of Sweden," the "President of
     Guatemala," and the "Turkish Public Library."

Reader, this will be a "perennial reminder"
Of the people (or such of them as pass the Secret Committee)
Who "fashioned this Canada of ours,"
For "One does not live only for toil and gain,"
Not, anyway, in First Families. It is comforting to believe
That while we "walk the earth," and pay $125,
And "after we have passed on," there will remain
"In the literature of the Universe," and particularly in the
     "Turkish Public Library,"
This "de luxe edition," "these unique and dignified annals,"
"These priceless and undying memories," with laudatory
     comments chosen by ourselves,
To which "succeeding First Families and historians alike will look,"
For "knowledge, guidance and inspiration."
Lives rich in eligibility will be "written large,"
(But within "a maximum of one thousand words")
"For all men to see and judge."
The "glorious dead," too,
These "selfless and noble defenders of Canada's honour,"
Will be incorporated in the Social Register

"Without any financial remuneration,"
Assuming, of course, that they are all
"Sons and daughters of its Members."

Reader, as you may guess, the Register
Was not "a spur of the moment idea."
It was "long and carefully nurtured,"
And "counsel was sought in high and authoritative places,"
So that it may "lay a basis upon which prominent Canadians will
     henceforth be appraised
As they go striding down the years,"
Paying their $125,
And receiving a "world-wide, gratuitous distribution,"
Even unto "the Turkish Public Library."

"Si monumentum requiris, circumspice!"
On this note, we both end.

[1954]

The Canadian Authors Meet

Expansive puppets percolate self-unction
Beneath a portrait of the Prince of Wales.
Miss Crotchet's muse has somehow failed to function,
Yet she's a poetess. Beaming, she sails

From group to chattering group, with such a dear
Victorian saintliness, as is her fashion,
Greeting the other unknowns with a cheer—
Virgins of sixty who still write of passion.

The air is heavy with Canadian topics,
And Carman, Lampman, Roberts, Campbell, Scott,
Are measured for their faith and philanthropics,
Their zeal for God and King, their earnest thought.

The cakes are sweet, but sweeter is the feeling
That one is mixing with the *literati*;
It warms the old, and melts the most congealing.
Really, it is a most delightful party.

Shall we go round the mulberry bush, or shall
We gather at the river, or shall we
Appoint a Poet Laureate this fall,
Or shall we have another cup of tea?

O Canada, O Canada, O can
A day go by without new authors springing
To paint the native maple, and to plan
More ways to set the selfsame welkin ringing?

[1927, rev. 1936, 1945, 1981]

Deleted final stanza, from the 1927 publication

Far in a corner sits (though none would know it)
The very picture of disconsolation,
A rather lewd and most ungodly poet
Writing these verses, for his soul's salvation.

[*McGill Fortnightly Review* 1927]

Bonne Entente

("One man's meat is another man's poisson." A. Lismer)

The advantages of living with two cultures
Strike one at every turn,
Especially when one finds a notice in an office building:
"This elevator will not run on Ascension Day";
Or reads in the *Montreal Star*:
"Tomorrow being the Feast of the Immaculate Conception,
There will be no collection of garbage in the city";
Or sees on the restaurant menu the bilingual dish:

DEEP APPLE PIE
TARTE AUX POMMES PROFONDES

[1954]

Brébeuf and His Brethren

When de Brébeuf and Lalemant, brave souls,
Were dying by the slow and dreadful coals
Their brother Jesuits in France and Spain
Were burning heretics with equal pain.
For both the human torture made a feast:
Then is priest savage, or Red Indian priest?

[1957]

All the Spikes But the Last

Where are the coolies in your poem, Ned?
Where are the thousands from China who swung their picks with
    bare hands at forty below?

Between the first and the million other spikes they drove, and the
    dressed-up act of Donald Smith, who has sung their story?

Did they fare so well in the land they helped to unite? Did they
    get one of the 25,000,000 CPR acres?

Is all Canada has to say to them written in the Chinese
    Immigration Act?

[1957]

Saturday Sundae

The triple-decker and the double-cone
I side-swipe swiftly, suck the Coke-straws dry.
Ride toadstool seat beside the slab of morgue—
Sweet corner drugstore, sweet pie in the sky.

Him of the front-flap apron, him I sing,
The counter-clockwise clerk in underalls.
Swing low, sweet chocolate, Oh swing, swing,
While cheek by juke the jitter chatter falls.

I swivel on my axle and survey
The latex tintex kotex cutex land.
Soft kingdoms sell for dimes, Life Pic Look Click
Inflate the male with conquest girly grand.

My brothers and my sisters, two by two,
Sit sipping succulence and sighing sex.
Each tiny adolescent universe
A world the vested interests annex.

Such bread and circuses these times allow,
Opium most popular, life so small and slick,
Perhaps with candy is the new world born
And cellophane shall wrap the heretic.

[1945]

Martinigram

The key person in the whole business
I said raising my Martini damn that woman
she didn't look where she was going sorry
it won't stain the key person what? oh it's
you Georgina no I won't be there tomorrow
see you some day the key person in the whole
business is not the one oh hello James yes
we're having a wonderful time not the one you
love but it's no thank you no more just now
not the one you love but it's the one who
does the hell's bells there's a stone in my olive

[1954]

A Lass in Wonderland

I went to bat for the Lady Chatte
　　Dressed in my bib and gown.
The judges three glared down at me
　　The priests patrolled the town.

My right hand shook as I reached for that book
　　And rose to play my part.
For out on the street were the marching feet
　　Of the League of the Sacred Heart.

The word "obscene" was supposed to mean
　　"Undue exploitation of sex."
This wording's fine for your needs and mine
　　But it's far too free for Quebec's.

I tried my best, with unusual zest,
　　To drive my argument through.
But I soon got stuck on what rhymes with "muck"
　　And that dubious word "undue."

So I raised their sights to the Bill of Rights
　　And cried: "Let freedom ring!"
Showed straight from the text that freedom of sex
　　Was as clear as anything.

Then I plunged into love, the spell that it wove,
　　And its attributes big and bold
Till the legal elect all stood erect
　　As my rapturous tale was told.

The judges' sighs and rolling of eyes
　　Gave hope that my case was won,
Yet Mellors and Connie still looked pretty funny
　　Dancing about in the sun.

What hurt me was not that they did it a lot
   And even ran out in the rain,
'Twas those curious poses with harebells and roses
   And that dangling daisy-chain.

Then too the sales made in the paperback trade
   Served to aggravate judicial spleen,
For it seems a high price will make any book nice
   While its mass distribution's obscene.

Oh Letters and Law are found in the raw
   And found on the heights sublime,
But D.H. Lawrence would view with abhorrence
   This Jansenist pantomime.

[1964]

Picture in "Life"

Here is a child, a small American girl-child, age fourteen,
Who has shot a lion. In Africa.
Far from her home in Morristown, New Jersey.
And she has shot a gnu, a wart-hog, and an elephant.
How shall we deal with her? Sir John Myrtle-Jenkinson
Shot lions in Africa in the days of the British,
But he was building an Empire. It was a man's job,
And he was a man, firm and philistine,
The Rule of Law in the deepest jungle,
And a black tie in a crisis.
Even the lions were proud
To pose with him for the *Illustrated London News*.
His was no idle slaughter, but the planting of the Flag,
The erection of the Cross, and the sale of cotton pants.
But this slip of a girl was on holiday from school.
She had not yet entered grade ten.
She killed innocently, unconsciously, as a tourist
Might stop to buy a postcard of Notre Dame.
She does not understand her summer trip
Dries up the sources of the fabulous Nile
And shoots great holes through all the myths of Europe.

[1954]

On Kanbawza Road

In Southeast Asia
  the Buddhist New Year
    starts with a water festival
     lasting for days

Everything is put aside
  for this glorification
    of rebirth

Even the guerillas
  who regularly cut the water-main
    into Rangoon
      promised no damage to the pipe-line
        during these celebrations

Only astrologers can tell
  the exact moment
    when the god descends
     and the year is born

A gun booms out their message

And walking by the Kanbawza Hotel
  on that bright morning
    under a torrid sun

I approached a gate on the roadway
  where stood a girl-child
    not three feet high
      holding a bowl of water
       with a spray
         of the sacred tha-bye tree

She too was celebrating
　　she was waiting to sprinkle
　　　　each passerby
　　　　　　with the symbolic drops

But I　　　I was a white man
　　standing so far above her
　　　　not easy to anoint

She moved toward me
　　then drew back
　　　　afraid

She understood the ritual
　　taught in her family
　　　　but never dreamed a foreign giant
　　　　　　might need her blessing

Seeing her torn
　　between faith and fear
　　　　I sat down on my heels
　　　　　　Burmese fashion
　　　　　　　　levelling my eyes with her eyes

And once her fear vanished
　　she smiled at me
　　　　her little hands
　　　　　　dipped the sprig in the bowl
　　　　　　　　and touched me with the fertility of love

[1962, 1978]

On the Death of Gandhi

India, India, I dreamed of your texture,
When a bullet, large as an army, tore through your heart.
The chord that broke loosened the holy rivers
And all the teeming lands were flooded with tears.

Your great one
Was close as though I could see and receive him.
Far away among my Canadian snows
The white of my landscape was tinged with his colour,
My mountains were taller.

I saw his road point to the goal of our freedom,
And I knew that we must aim
At the centre of his terrible simplicity
Or be condemned in our darkness to cower
Behind the walls of our little religions,
Shrinking from the shadow of our own untouchables.

This is my salute
To the towering truth of his vision:
Though evil had power to draw off his praying blood,
The doors of his temple have opened on all the world.

India, India, the load of your history
Presses down upon the springs of your progress,
For man is heir of his past, yet his spirit
Leaps, in an instant, over the Himalayas.

[1954]

For Bryan Priestman

(Drowned while attempting to save a child)

The child fell, turning slowly with arms outstretched like a doll,
One shrill cry dying under the arches,
And floated away, her time briefer than foam.

Nothing was changed on the summer's day. The birds sang,
The busy insects followed their fixed affairs.
Only a Professor of Chemistry, alone on the bridge,
Suddenly awoke from his reverie, into the intense moment,
Saw all the elements of his life compounded for testing,
And plunged with searching hands into his last experiment.

This was a formula he had carried from childhood,
That can work but once in the life of a man.
His were the labels of an old laboratory,
And the long glass tubes of the river.

[1954]

Last Rites

Within his tent of pain and oxygen
This man is dying; grave, he mutters prayers,
Stares at the bedside altar through the screens,
Lies still for invocation and for hands.
Priest takes his symbols from a leather bag.
Supplice and stole, the pyx and marks of faith,
And makes a chancel in the ether air.
Nurse too is minister. Tall cylinders,
Her altar-boys, press out rich draughts for lungs
The fluid slowly fills. The trick device
Keeps the worn heart from failing, and bright dials
Flicker their needles as the pressures change,
Like eyelids on his eyes. Priest moves in peace,
Part of his other world. Nurse prays with skills,
Serving her Lord with rites and acts of love.
Both acolytes are uniformed in white
And wear a holy look, for both are near
The very point and purpose of their art.
Nurse is precise and careful. She will fail
In the end, and lose her battle. Death will block
The channels of her aid, and brush aside
All her exact inventions, leaving priest
Triumphant on his ground. But nurse will stare
This evil in the face, will not accept,
Will come with stranger and more cunning tools
To other bedsides, adding skill to skill,
Till death is driven slowly farther back.
How far? She does not ask.
                              Priest does not fight.
He lives through death and death is proof of him.
In the perpetual, unanswerable why
Are born the symbol and the sacrifice.
The warring creeds run past the boundary
And stake their claims to heaven; science drives

The boundary back, and claims the living land,
A revelation growing, piece by piece,
Wonder and mystery as true as God.
And I who watch this rightness and these rites,
I see my father in the dying man,
I am his son who dwells upon the earth,
There is a holy spirit in this room,
And straight toward me from both sides of time
Endless the known and unknown roadways run.

[1954]

Ushering in the Quiet Revolution
(From the Quebec Liberal Party's election pamphlet)
1960

J.- OMER DIONNE
Candidat pour le comté de COMPTON
(complete description)

Agriculteur, 55 ans,
10 enfants.
Membre de la Ligue du Sacré-Coeur.
Une soeur religieuse,
Supérieure d'un hôpital au Nouveau-Brunswick;
Deux cousins missionaires,
Son neveu est curé
De St. Alcide.

Frédéric COITEUX
Candidat pour l'Assomption
(complete description)

Cultivateur, 58 ans,
10 enfants,
Vice-prés. de l'Office
Des Marchés des Tabacs du Québec.
Membre de la Ligue du Sacré-Coeur
Et marguillier.
Un fils, clerc de St. Viateur,
Une fille religieuse au Mont-Jésus-Marie,
Une fille Oblate de Marie-Immaculée.

[1967]

Audacity

(*"Audacity is missing in Canada."* The *Times* 30/11/59)

They say we lack audacity, that we are middle class, without the
adventurousness that arises from the desperation of the lower
classes or the tradition of the upper classes.
They say we are more emphatically middling than any country
west of Switzerland, and that boldness and experiment are far
from our complacent thoughts.
But I say to you, they do not know where to look, and have not
the eyes to see.
For audacity is all around us,
Boldness sits in the highest places,
We are riddled with insolence.

Do you want audacity?
Let me tell you—
Any day in Montreal you may hear the guns crack at the
noon-hour, as the police give chase to the bank-robbers
Who are helping themselves to the wealth of the land like the
French and the English before them, *coureur de bois* and
fur-trader rolled into one;
You may watch the patrol cars circle their beats to gather the
weekly pay-off from unlicensed cafés
Whose owners sell booze on the side to acquire the $15,000 they
need for the $25-permit;
You may learn the name of the distinguished Legislative
Councillor who controls the *caisse-électorale*
Into which rattles the coin that makes possible the letting of
contracts,
And who tips his hat to the priest
And is saluted respectfully in return;
You may marvel at the boldness of promoters of oil and natural
gas, men too quick for production, fixers and peddlers,
Getting their hands on concessions and rights, access to

underground treasures awaiting man's use in the womb of
    our northland,
Playing the suckers and markets, turning their thousands to
    millions, loading the pipe-lines with overhead that is paid by
    the housewife who cooks her spaghetti,
Then solemnly demanding higher rates for sales of the product
    (extra hot, natural gas!) before friends on the Board of
    Control:
You may follow the hucksters and admen compiling their
    budgets, planning the assault on "public opinion," setting the
    poll-questions,
Writing editorials for weeklies, letters to editors, telegrams to
    senators, articles for journals,
Day after day on the job of confusing the issue, baiting the
    eggheads, laughing at the "culture kids" of CBC, fixing the
    give-aways,
Posing as democracy's friends and admirers, while undermining
    the concept of government and welfare,
Singing the praises of free enterprise that relies on high tariffs,
    defence contracts and floor prices;
You may stand in awe at the audacity of journalists, twisting the
    news items by headline and rewrite, blanking out truth,
Ponderously laying down the conventional wisdom in
    unconventional English,
While a few owners gather dailies into chains run by gangs of
    paid hack-men,
Then add on the radio stations and TV outlets, lest some glimmer
    of free opinion escape them;
You may be amazed at the boldness of churchmen and ministers,
    meeting in synod and conclave and conference to spy out our
    sinfulness,
Who wax indignant over lotteries, horse-racing and the drink
    question, or, with Savonarola intensity,
Denounce crime-comics and short bathing-suits;
But all this is as nothing, not worthy of mention,
Beside the supreme, the breath-taking audacity
Of the great executives in their panelled boardrooms

Found at every point in the social structure where policy is laid
    down or decision taken,
Without whom no hospital can be opened, no charitable
    campaign launched, no church can engage a preacher and no
    university can build a building,
Daring to be omniscient, omnipotent, omnipresent, not to
    mention omnivorous—
These surely you can see in this Canada of ours, O London
    Times,
In this country that has the audacity to proclaim the "supremacy
    of God"
In its Bill of Rights?

[1964]

Fort Smith

The town siren went off
And everyone looked for the fire.
Kids from every corner
Bounded like little wolves,
While adults stood around
Grinning at the false alarm
As cars and trucks rolled up
With a grand old fire-pump.
Looking about the crowd
I saw a collar reversed,
The white circle of my childhood,
And a gentle Anglican face
In the modest clergyman's dress.

The Rev. Burt Evans
Picked us out as strangers
And offered to show us around
In his new Volkswagen.
So we shoved aside a baby-crib
And filled up the Nazi car
To explore Canada's colony.
There was the Bank of Commerce
In a new tar-paper bunk-house
Opened six days ago,
The Hudson's Bay Store and Hotel,
Government Offices, Liquor Store,
RCMP Headquarters, Catholic Hospital,
Anglican and Catholic Churches,
The Imperial Oil Compound,
The Barber Shop and Pool Room,
A weedy golf course, the Curling Club,
And the Uranium Restaurant, full of young people
Playing song-hits on the juke-box.

We drove on sandy streets.
No names yet, except "Axe-handle Road."
There was the "native quarter,"
Shacks at every angle
For Slave Indians and half-breeds,
And overlooking the river
The trim houses of the civil servants
With little lawns and gardens
And tents for children to play Indian in.

The Rev. Burt Evans
Stopped his car by a Grotto
Close to the Catholic Church.
Rocks had been piled in a heap
To make a cave for the Virgin.
Flags had been draped across
And benches were neatly placed.
"This has an appeal," he said,
"To the superstitious element in the population,"
And sighed a little, as one might,
Who knew it was not quite cricket.

We climbed down to the Slave
To the rock polished by ice
And the roar of the great rapids.
This is the edge of the Shield—
Eastward, away to Labrador,
Lies the pre-Cambrian rock,
While North and South and West
Stretches the central plain
Unbroken from Gulf to Arctic,
Hemmed in by the western hills.
Three boys came out of a hideaway
And showed us fresh tracks of moose.

Pierre, suddenly challenged,
Stripped and walked into the rapids,
Firming his feet against rock,
Standing white, in white water,
Leaning south up the current
To stem the downward rush,
A man testing his strength
Against the strength of his country.

[1973]

A New City: E3

Now Indian and Eskimo watch
The slow, inescapable death
Of this land which has waited so long
For the sentence already pronounced.
America's overspill
Invades the tundra and lakes
Extracting, draining away,
Leaving a slum behind,
Spreading its colour and shape
Like brown water on snow.

But wait! A new city is planned
Across from Aklavik's mud,
Free from the perma-frost,
Set upon solid rock,
Blue-printed, pre-fab, precise,
A model, a bureaucrat's dream.
Here we went to observe
The first Council meeting
North of the Arctic Circle,
The birth of democracy
Swaddled in ancient dress,
Where the Commissioner and nine whites
(Four elected and five named)
Came to ratify laws
Pre-cast in Ottawa.
The two of us, looking on,
With a priest in a black soutane,
And the RCMP in its braid
Were all the public around,
No Indian or Eskimo face.

All was in doubt at the start.
The Mace, where was the Mace?
The massive, Massey Mace
Weighing two hundred pounds?
A most magnificent Mace
Fashioned of local stuff,
Indian beads, and the tusk
Of a narwhal, Eskimo stone,
And copper from a Franklin kettle
Set in the crest of a Crown.
Alas, the Mace ran aground
Crossing the Delta flats
In a high-speed motor boat,
Somewhere out in the murk
Where only the musk-rat thrives.

Symbols are magic, and work
As well in idea as in fact.
The Great Seal dropped in the Thames
By a fleeing Jacobite King
Hindered not Parliament,
Nor the lack of the Mace this meet.
For now an obedient voice
Carefully coached in advance
Solemnly rose to speak:
"I move that we proceed
In the absence of the Mace
As if the Mace were here."
Carried unanimously!—
The gap in the ritual
Covered by common sense.

[1973]

On Saying Goodbye to My Room
in Chancellor Day Hall

Rude and rough men are invading my sanctuary.
They are carting away all my books and papers.
My pictures are stacked in an ugly pile in the corner.
       There is murder in my cathedral.

The precious files, filled with yesterday's writing,
The letters from friends long dead, the irreplaceable evidence
Of battles now over, or worse, still in full combat—
       Where are they going? How shall I find them again?

Miserable vandals, stuffing me into your cartons,
This is a functioning office, all things are in order,
Or in that better disorder born of long usage.
       I alone can command it.

I alone know the secret thoughts in these cabinets,
And how the letters relate to the pamphlets in boxes.
I alone know the significance of underlinings
       On the pages read closely.

You scatter these sources abroad, and who then shall use them?
Oh, I am told, they will have a small place in some basement.
Gladly some alien shelves in a distant library
       Will give them safe shelter.

But will there be pictures of J.S. Woodsworth and Coldwell
Above the Supreme Court Reports? The Universal Declaration
Of Human Rights, will it be found hanging
       Near the left-wing manifestos?

And where are the corners to hold all the intimate objects
Gathered over the rich, the incredible years?
The sprig of cedar, the segment of Boulder Dam cable,
The heads of Buddha and Dante, the concretions, the arrowheads,
   Where, where will they be?

Or the clock that was taken from my 1923 air-cooled Franklin?
The cardboard Padlock, a gift from awakened students?
The Oxford oar, the Whitefield Quebec, the Lorcini?
   These cry out my history.

These are all cells to my brain, a part of my total.
Each filament thought feeds them into the process
By which we pursue the absolute truth that eludes us.
   They shared my decisions.

Now they are going, and I stand again on new frontiers.
Forgive this moment of weakness, this backward perspective.
Old baggage, I wish you goodbye and good housing.
   I strip for more climbing.

[1973]

Villanelle for Our Time

From bitter searching of the heart,
Quickened with passion and with pain
We rise to play a greater part.

This is the faith from which we start:
Men shall know commonwealth again
From bitter searching of the heart.

We loved the easy and the smart,
But now, with keener hand and brain,
We rise to play a greater part.

The lesser loyalties depart,
And neither race nor creed remain
From bitter searching of the heart.

Not steering by the venal chart
That tricked the mass for private gain,
We rise to play a greater part.

Reshaping narrow law and art
Whose symbols are the millions slain,
From bitter searching of the heart
We rise to play a greater part.

[1945]

Afterword

Reading "Canon" Scott's Canon

Born in 1899 in the Rectory of St. Matthew's Church in Quebec City, the son of a clergyman poet, Francis Reginald Scott never did stray far from the precincts of Christianity, no matter how much his verse countenances both penicillin and V.I. Lenin, science and social reform, and bids us create a heaven here and now. Indeed, from his father—Frederick George Scott (1861–1944), a dissenting Protestant and a social radical—F.R. Scott seems to have inherited the ideal that the role of a godly soul in the Age of Progress, Revolution, and Anxiety is to agitate for intelligent and compassionate legislation and to lampoon those who credit that the Golden Rule is the rule of gold. Similarly, rather than treat God's Word as sacrosanct, Scott views the Book of Genesis via Charles Darwin, the Song of Solomon as illustrated by Aubrey Beardsley, and the Book of Revelation as interpreted by Karl Marx. The filial Scott's critique of ruling-class inhumanity—and inanity—issues, thus, as polite, if politic, satire. His "agenda" poetry never prods us to storm the Bastille; it asks us to spurn peerages and the soirees of derelict poetesses. The gent is a brilliant, "light" poet (think Noel Coward with an Oxford degree and a "bleeding heart")—whose lyrics elicit the knowing nod and the wry smile. Too, his work is often "occasional," logging responses to incidents involving ridiculous plutocrats, poets gone politically awry, "recovered" discourses that satirize themselves, and natural events that invite a moral (as with Christ's teachings). Formally, Scott's verse consists of secular sermons (especially the "found" poems), parables, and proverbs, most touched with satire or couched in irony. Confirming the religious impulse of his thought, Scott is most closeted on self and sex. Naked autobiography is just as obscured as are bare-naked limbs. Yes, the settings of poems allow us to imagine an intimate acquaintance with Scott's persona(e); but eroticism is spirited into landscape. Hence, Scott's Modernism is rendered *responsible* in a Victorian, bourgeois manner: he won't decapitate capitalists; he seeks their rehab; he doesn't garb nude Venus in sackcloth; he styles her as Mother Earth. (Instead of odes to bedding beauties, Scott posits the beauties of bedrock—a righteously Anglo-Canadian notion of "hard-core.") Unlike Sade, he doesn't ejaculate in the faces of prudes. Not Mao; he doesn't mow down landlords. He chafes against propriety and he complains about potentates, but the charges are always temperate, good-humoured, *respectable*—as befit a barrister, a professor, and a *son of the cloth*.

According to Brian Trehearne, the contradictions between Scott the Socialist Modernist and Scott the Victorian may be resolved if we allow for the influence, on the "early" Scott, of Aestheticism (the pursuit of *la poésie pure*) and Decadence (the use of emphatic imagery of decay to elaborate themes of imperilled *Beauty* and atheist *angst*). These tendencies exist, but it may also be that socially conscious *Faith*, if never explicitly articulated, serves as Scott's most faithful guide.

In "The Canadian Authors Meet" (1927), first published in *The McGill Fortnightly Review*, Scott's terminal stanza (often omitted from anthologies), runs:

Far in a corner sits (though none would know it)
The very picture of disconsolation,
A rather lewd and most ungodly poet
Writing these verses, for his soul's salvation.

Trehearne views the self-portrait of the "lewd" and "ungodly" poet as a typical Decadent statement. Yet this virtual confession is merely a secularization of, say, St. Augustine's admissions of lust and doubt. Instead of writing an outright prayer, Scott pens "verses" to win, not Christian "salvation," no, but admission to the Pantheon. Indeed, this last stanza is a pointed answer to the poem's opening parade of "Expansive puppets [who] percolate self-unction": these self-appointed bards are poseurs, who exude a faux "Victorian saintliness" and deign to judge superior poets according to their "faith and philanthropics, / Their zeal for God and King." Intriguingly, Scott's persona is that of the outlaw saint who exposes the hypocrisies and the pretentiousness of other clerics (here, poetasters) while recognizing his own alleged "sins." Indeed, that self-flagellation verifies his authenticity. Again, the model seems Augustinian. Scott is the true poet, whose own "self-unction" is, ironically, his indirect praise of his veracity and his fidelity to "real" poetry. (Note that "self" is a crucial word in this poem: criticism of false poets' self-flattery, use of rhetoric ["selfsame"], and self-conscious archaisms ["welkin"] culminate in the persona's own self-salvation as an isolated, disconsolate misfit, that is to say, as performing as a good—and thus "ungodly," given present company—poet.) The Canadian Authors gather, sip their tea, and lisp their verities, but off in a corner—like Christ in the desert—is the veritable Messiah of Anglo-Canadian verse, exposing the black-ties and the bluestockings as Philistines, while he himself, one of the frank-talking Elect, inks the truths and confessions that fine poetry demands.

Admittedly, "frank" is a handy pun above, but it is not inconsequential that Francis/Frank Scott signed some of his early verse "F.R.S.": he would have known that his initials are also an acronym denoting a "Fellow of the Royal Society."[1] Thus, there is a prankish side to Scott's wit (cf. his tongue-in-cheek "curating" of "found" poems) that suits the Decadent heritage of the "dandy" in literature and the harlequin in art. But the prankster or "Fool" is also, classically, the kingdom's loyal speaker of truth—though delivered as jest. Scott—as "Fellow of a Royal Society"—assumed his position, not due to social rank (which would be "rank"), but due to his self-election as a jester-outcast, pointing fingers at various kings *sans culottes*, priests without conscience, economists without hearts, and poets without brains.

One fine example of Scott's practice is "Saturday Sundae" (1945), where the poet chastises "free enterprise" for commercializing experiences of Judeo-Christian Sabbath "rest" ("Saturday" or Sunday—echoed in "Sundae") and secularizing once-sacred satisfactions (sex, nourishment, and worship). Scott doesn't skewer a bare-assed emperor but an entire socio-economic complex: the "seduction of the innocent"[2] (youths) into godless consumerism. The "him" sung here is neither Him nor hymn but a soda jerk—the "counter-clockwise clerk." From the progressive, epic, religious struggle that ended slavery and gave the world "Negro spirituals," there remains now only, in effect, an advertising slogan: "Swing low, sweet chocolate . . ." No divine chariot will transport us to heaven: instead, we now inherit the "Soft kingdom" of a chocolate sundae. Scott's jester persona observes:

My brothers and my sisters, two by two,
Sit sipping succulence and sighing sex.
Each tiny adolescent universe
A world the vested interests annex.

These naive citizens are rendered docile and impotent ("sighing sex")—conquered—by an Orwellian Big Brother who tames them by feeding (but not truly satisfying) their desires. In North America, unscathed by global war's wanton devastation, both Marxist class struggle and apocalyptic Christianity have been rendered null and void by "bread and circuses," that is, merchandise and merchandising. In the so-called New World, this is how "the new world" (a reference to Aldous Huxley's satirical novel *Brave New World* [1932]) is born—"with candy" and, gift-wrapped in cellophane, "the heretic." In the poem, Scott is the "heretic"—the "Holy Fool." Or he is, as in "The Canadian Authors Meet," an "ungodly poet": the iconoclastic clairvoyant who castigates the backward, the perverse, and, the unholy. "Saturday Sundae" is, really, a witty sermon.

Ditto for the rhyming couplets of "Mural" (1945), which follows "Saturday Sundae" in lamenting a world where Technology and Commerce have displaced Nature and Religion:

When shepherds cease to watch their flocks
And tend instead bacterial stocks;

. . . .

When ova swell in Huxleyan tubes,
Paternal sperm is sold in cubes,

. . . .

Then poverty shall be a word
Philologists alone have heard,
The slightest want shall know its fill,
Desire shall culminate in skill.
The carefree lovers shall repair
To halls of air-conditioned air
And tune-in coloured symphonies
To prick their elongated bliss.

Although this poem declares its indebtedness to British author Aldous Huxley (1894–1963), the argument anticipates by two decades *Lament for a Nation: The Defeat of Canadian Nationalism* (1965), by George Grant (1918–88), a conservative Canadian Christian philosopher who warns that the wedding of godless liberalism and amoral technology will erect a global tyranny. Scott's poem prophesies this nightmarish future, wherein humanity's propensity for violence will be "streamlined into zeal / For one colossal commonweal." It is his subtle Christian humanist critique of modernity that allows Socialist Scott an intellectual alignment with the "Red Tory" Grant.

Though they mock Christians who are sycophants to wealth or who scorn scientific progress and conveniences, Scott's "found" poems are also ironic— yet subtly religious—commentaries. In "Bonne Entente" (1954), a poem that chuckles at comic juxtapositions—or translations—of French and English cultures in Montreal, Scott's examples are striking: in an office tower, a sign declares, "This elevator will not run on Ascension Day"; on "the Feast of the Immaculate Conception / There will be no collection of garbage . . ." These "finds" illustrate the disjuncture between an officially pious Québécois Catholic state and the needs of commercial, industrial urbanity.[3] Scott's analysis seems opposite to that posited in "Saturday Sundae," save that there he attacks the insidious intent of Big Business to replace *Faith* with shopping; and here he ridicules the disturbingly comic-cum-anti-democratic fusion of church and state in a scandalously feudal Quebec. (The poem's final joke, playing on the difference between an apple pie that is "DEEP" as opposed to a pie featuring apples that are "PROFONDES"/profound, renders palatable the scathing, preceding jests.) Although "Bonne Entente" can be read as a secular-ist critique, it also echoes Christ's teaching (one popular with "work ethic" Protestants) that common sense should sometimes supersede doctrine: "Which of you shall have an ass or an ox fallen into a pit, and will not straightway pull him out [even] on the sabbath day?" (Luke 14: 5).[4] Once again, then, Scott plays the "Holy Fool," underlining diabolical absurdity.

True: Scott never professes belief in these poems; he cannot. Rather, he articulates his Christianity by using its residual, moral strictures to prod society to palliate triumph-of-the-richest policies with communalist, social-democratic laws and acts. Thus, as a public intellectual, Scott participates in the formation of the League for Social Reconstruction (1932)—a leftist think tank—and helps to organize the Co-operative Commonwealth Federation (1935), the democratic socialist party that eventually introduced publicly funded health care to Canada. As a lawyer, he promotes civil rights and constitutional reform—and mentors Pierre Elliott Trudeau (1918–2000), the future prime minister of Canada (1968–79, 1980–84), who will enshrine a bill of rights in a new constitution (1982). In the arts, Scott is an architect of the McGill Movement and a co-editor of the signal anthology *New Provinces: Poems of Several Authors* (1936), as well as a prime mover behind several modernizing Anglo-Canadian "little magazines." Arguably, Scott channels the Victorian Christian Progressivism of his parents into social(ist) "good works" and into backing a "modern(ist)" poetry of political engagement.

Treharne elaborates Scott's affiance with late-Victorian Aestheticism and Decadence, while other scholars delineate Scott's debt to the Anglo-American High Modernists—T.S. Eliot (1888–1965) and Ezra Pound (1885–1972)—as well as Scott's tutelage by his McGill University mate A.J.M. Smith (1902–80). One cannot refute any of these influences: Eliot's Prufrock shadows Scott's persona among the Canadian Authors; Pound's Mauberley haunts the commentaries offered in "Saturday Sundae" and "Mural." Too, as Smith produces his acerbic, urbane quatrains and *vers libre* paeans to Nature, so does Scott jot his own. Yet Scott dissents from Eliot and Pound because he has a sense of humour, or rather is less apocalyptic. For him, the Great War wasn't the wreck of civilization; rather, the *idea* of the Russian Revolution and the possibility for global, socioeconomic development are harbingers of potential good—if the *right* people take command and if they do the *right* things. While *frère* Canuck Smith lauds our native wilderness as "the beauty / of strength / broken by strength / and still strong" ("The Lonely Land" [1936]), Scott prefers to depict "Pierre" (Trudeau) "testing his strength / Against the strength of his country" ("Fort Smith" [1973]). Scott is more practical, then, and less an aesthete than is Smith.

Scott's poetry suggests other influences too. The Rhodes Scholar was surely conversant with contemporary British poetry;[5] and he was a McGill student when Montreal was the city to be in for any liquor-loving Yank during the US Prohibition years. Presumably, then, Scott encountered more than one thirsty American intellectual, and must have imbibed *Poetry*, the Chicago-based magazine that was the Bible of US Modernism (with Pound as its "foreign correspondent"). In its pages, Scott would have read Carl Sandburg (1878–1967), a disciple of Walt Whitman (1819–92) but no wide-eyed mystic, a people's poet but no propagandist. Sandburg's "The People, Yes" (1936), with its talk of "hands [that] milked, hands [that] husked and harnessed," looks forward to Scott's "Laurentian Shield" (1954), which predicts the arrival of northern settlers "whose hands can turn . . . rock into children." Scott's "Audacity" (1964) is also reminiscent of Sandburg, especially the latter's "Good Morning, America" (1928). Scott's "Martinigram" (1954) may echo Sandburg's own experiments with "overheard" speech, such as "Snatch of Sliphorn Jazz" (1928), while Scott's "Picture in 'Life'" (1954) is the same breed of anecdote that Sandburg well employs, as in "The People, Yes": "'Why,' said the Denver Irish policeman as he / arrested a Pawnee Indian I.W.W. soapboxer, / 'why don't you go back where you came from?'"

Another major influence for Scott is undoubtedly E.J. Pratt (1882–1964), a Newfoundland-born Anglo-Canadian English professor and ordained Methodist minister whose humanist poetry has no quarrel with evolution or other scientific scripture. Indeed, Pratt seems to regard Christianity as a noble, superior superstition, for its claim to arise from the martyrdom of a God-conceived Man serves to render humanity more humane. Thus, Pratt's "Come Away, Death" (1943) refers to the "outmoded page of the Apocalypse"; his "The Truant" (1943) depicts courageous, inventive Man as heroically defying a tyrannical and passé god. Pratt's "From Stone to Steel" (1932) views humanity as evolving technologically, yes; but spiritually, only fitfully, from paganism to Christianity. Pratt's influence on Scott is visible in the younger poet's endorsements of evolutionary struggle and scientific advancement. See Scott's "Coelacanth" (1964), "My Amoeba Is Unaware" (1954), "Lakeshore" (1954), and "Incident at May Pond" (1964). But Scott also answers Pratt's nationalist epics, *Brébeuf and His Brethren* (1940) and *Towards the Last Spike* (1952). Where Pratt salutes the 1649 martyrdom of Brébeuf and another French settler-cleric at Saint-Ignace, Huronia (present-day Simcoe County, Ontario) by the Iroquois, proposing that the European deaths served the civilizing mission of Christianity, Scott differs. In his radically succinct "Brébeuf and His Brethren" (1957), Scott reminds Pratt that, if "Red Indian" was playing torturer and terrorist here, so were "Jesuits in France and Spain" perpetrating horrors there. Our "Holy Fool" shows up grotesque hypocrisy. Pratt's *Towards the Last Spike* epicizes the construction of Canada's coast-to-coast railway, and chooses Nature and politicos as its heroes, thus omitting the Chinese labourers who did drive into numberless railway ties "All the Spikes But the Last" (1957), to cite Scott's title. Scott employs a kind of Whitman/Sandburg-biblical verse-line to answer "Ned" Pratt's blank verse, thus visibly setting his own populism against the former's elitism. But as much as his defence of the "coolie" is welcome, Scott's primary purpose is to duel with a poet peer, *not* to salvage or to assert the rights of Chinese Canadians.

One other probable vital model for Scott is British: W.H. Auden (1907–73). From Auden (as from Sandburg), Scott likely adopted the view that a poet should be "a bit of a reporter," and so make poetry of economic hardship and socio-political challenges (qtd. in Allott 20). So, Scott's elegy "For Bryan Priestman" (1954) and its line "Nothing was changed on the summer day" owe something to Auden's "Musée des Beaux-Arts" (1940) and its lines "the sun shone / as it had to" as "everything turn[ed] away / Quite leisurely from the disaster." Like Auden (and Pratt), too, Scott can ink a gay, Latinate quatrain ("On Saying Goodbye to My Room in Chancellor Day Hall" [1973]) or sly couplets ("Ode to a Politician" [1942]) to articulate a point.

Scott is an excellent poet, not across his oeuvre but in verses that exemplify specific forms. He echoes other poets with craft and facility, but he equals his tutors only haphazardly, when momentous event—or inspiration—transpires. Ultimately, the canonical Scott is an expert formalist: The Poet of the Epigram. Still, he's constrained—by a duty to protest injustice without being unjust; and by a duty to be circumspect, thus circumscribing personality. But one loves Scott most when he is most frank, most joyous—as in "Orangerie" (1973); "On Kanbawza Road" (1962, 1978), with its debt to the travel lyrics of Br'er Canuck bard Earle Birney (1904–95); and "Miranda" (1926), a poem whose singing puts an end to preaching.

—*George Elliott Clarke*

Notes

1 Scott became a Fellow of the Royal Society of Canada in 1947.

2 I nod to Wertham.

3 The found poem "Ushering in the Quiet Revolution" (1967) makes a similar point. Yet the true irony in a poem that models Catholic agrarians as unlikely radicals is that these were the very people who did in fact modernize and secularize Quebec society in the 1960s.

4 See also Scott's "A New City: E3" (1973), where a political meeting proceeds without a ceremonial mace because the participants vote to act "in the absence of the Mace / As if the Mace were here." Thus, "The gap in the ritual / [Was] Covered by common sense."

5 Surely inspiration for *New Provinces* were the British anthologies *New Signatures* (1932) and *New Country* (1933), both edited by Michael Roberts, a champion of activist verse. Scott likely also knew *New Verse*, a UK "little magazine"-cum-anthology founded in 1933 and edited by Geoffrey Grigson.

Works Cited

Allott, Kenneth. "Introductory Note." *The Penguin Book of Contemporary Verse.* Ed. Allott. 1950. Harmondsworth: Penguin, 1954. 11–27. Print.

Auden, W.H. "Musée des Beaux-Arts." *The Norton Anthology of Poetry: Revised.* Ed. Alexander W. Allison, et al. New York: Norton, 1975. 1116–17. Print.

Daymond, Douglas, and Leslie Monkman, eds. *Literature in Canada.* Vol. 2. Toronto: Gage, 1978. Print.

Grigson, Geoffrey, ed. *New Verse.* 1933–1939. Print.

Pratt, E.J. *Brébeuf and His Brethren.* 1940. *E.J. Pratt: Complete Poems.* Ed. Sandra Djwa and R.G. Moyles. Part 2. Toronto: U of Toronto P, 1989. 46–110. Print.

———. "Come Away, Death." Daymond and Monkman 15–16.

———. "From Stone to Steel." Daymond and Monkman 13–14.

———. *Towards the Last Spike.* Toronto: Macmillan, 1952. Print.

———. "The Truant." *The Oxford Book of Canadian Verse: In English and French.* Ed. A.J.M. Smith. Toronto: Oxford UP, 1960, 1961. 148–54. Print.

Roberts, Michael, ed. *New Country: Prose and Poetry by the Authors of New Signatures.* 1933. Hallandale, FL: New World, 1971. Print.

———, ed. *New Signatures: Poems by Several Hands.* 1932. London: L. & Virginia Woolf, 1935. Print. Hogarth Living Poets 24.

Sandburg, Carl. From "Good Morning, America." *Harvest* 77–80.

———. *Harvest Poems: 1910–1960.* New York: Harcourt, Brace, & World—Harvest, 1960. Print.

———. From "The People, Yes." *Harvest* 89–105.

———. "Snatch of Sliphorn Jazz." *Harvest* 86.

The Scofield Reference Bible. Ed. C.I. Scofield. 1909. Oxford: Oxford UP, 1917. Print.

Scott, F.R. "Ode to a Politician." *Overture.* Toronto: Ryerson, 1945. 32–34. Print.

Smith, A.J.M. "The Lonely Land." Daymond and Monkman 120.

Trehearne, Brian. *Aestheticism and The Canadian Modernists: Aspects of a Poetic Influence.* Kingston: McGill-Queen's UP, 1989. Print.

Wertham, Fredric. *The Seduction of the Innocent: The Influence of Comic Books on Today's Youth.* New York: Rinehart, 1954. Print.

Acknowledgements

The editors and the publisher gratefully acknowledge William Toye, the executor of F.R. Scott's estate, for his permission to republish the poems listed below.

From *McGill Fortnightly Review* 1.2 (1927)
    "The Canadian Authors Meet"

From *Overture* (Toronto: Ryerson, 1945).
    "The Canadian Authors Meet"

From *Events and Signals* (Toronto: Ryerson, 1954)
    "The Canadian Social Register"
    "Bonne Entente"
    "Laurentian Shield"

From *Signature* (Vancouver: Klanak, 1964)
    "Audacity"

From *The Eye of the Needle: Satire, Sorties, Sundries* (Montreal: Contact, 1957)
    "Social Notes I, 1932"
    "Social Notes II, 1935"
    "All the Spikes But the Last"

From *Trouvailles: Poems from Prose* (Montreal: Delta, 1967)
    "Ushering in the Quiet Revolution"

From *The Dance Is One* (Toronto: McClelland and Stewart, 1973)
    "A New City: E3"

From *The Collected Poems of F.R. Scott* (Toronto: McClelland and Stewart, 1981)
    "Overture"
    "Laurentian Shield"
    "Coelacanth"
    "Orangerie"
    "My Amoeba Is Unaware"
    "Mural"

"Lakeshore"
"A Grain of Rice"
"Incident at May Pond"
"Miranda"
"Trans Canada"
"To Certain Friends"
"Social Notes I, 1932"
"Social Notes II, 1935"
"Lest We Forget"
"For R.A.S. 1925–1943"
"W.L.M.K."
"The Canadian Social Register"
"The Canadian Authors Meet"
"Bonne Entente"
"Brébeuf and His Brethren"
"All the Spikes But the Last"
"Saturday Sundae"
"Martinigram"
"A Lass in Wonderland"
"Picture in 'Life'"
"On Kanbawza Road"
"On the Death of Gandhi"
"For Bryan Priestman"
"Last Rites"
"Ushering in the Quiet Revolution"
"Audacity"
"Fort Smith"
"A New City: E3"
"On Saying Goodbye to My Room in Chancellor Day Hall"
"Villanelle for Our Time"

Laura Moss would like to thank Neil Besner and Brian Henderson for being so committed to the series and to this project, Melanie Unrau for having such sharp editorial eyes, and George Elliott Clarke for coming on board and writing with such poetic passion. Thanks too, as always, to Fred, Simon, Owen, and Charlie.

Neil Besner would like to thank Melanie Unrau for her excellent editorial help with every facet of this volume's preparation and for her admirable commitment to the Laurier Poetry Series. I am also grateful to the EMIC (Editing Modernism in Canada) project for providing the funding for Melanie to work on this project.

lps Books in the Laurier Poetry Series
Published by Wilfrid Laurier University Press

Eli Mandel *From Room to Room: The Poetry of Eli Mandel*, edited by Peter Webb, with an afterword by Andrew Stubbs • 2011 • xviii + 66 pp. • ISBN 978-1-55458-255-6

Steve McCaffery *Verse and Worse: Selected and New Poems of Steve McCaffery 1989–2009*, edited by Darren Wershler, with an afterword by Steve McCaffery • 2010 • xiv + 76 pp. • ISBN 978-1-55458-188-7

Don McKay *Field Marks: The Poetry of Don McKay*, edited by Méira Cook, with an afterword by Don McKay • 2006 • xxvi + 60 pp. • ISBN-10: 0-88920-494-2; ISBN-13: 978-0-88920-494-2

Al Purdy *The More Easily Kept Illusions: The Poetry of Al Purdy*, edited by Robert Budde, with an afterword by Russell Brown • 2006 • xvi + 80 pp. • ISBN-10: 0-88920-490-X; ISBN-13: 978-0-88920-490-4

F.R. Scott *Leaving the Shade of the Middle Ground: The Poetry of F.R. Scott*, edited by Laura Moss, with an afterword by George Elliott Clarke • 2011 • xxiv + 72 pp. • ISBN 978-1-55458-367-6

Fred Wah *The False Laws of Narrative: The Poetry of Fred Wah*, edited by Louis Cabri, with an afterword by Fred Wah • 2009 • xxiv + 78 pp. • ISBN 978-1-555458-046-0